The Forgiveness Workshop
From Higher Self/Spirit

By Cat Baldwin

For permission, serialization, condensation, adaptions, or for our catalog of other publications, write to Ozark Mountain Publishing, Inc., P.O. Box 754, Huntsville, AR 72740, ATTN: Permissions Department.

Library of Congress Cataloging-in-Publication Data

Cat Baldwin -1958-

The Forgiveness Workshop by Cat Baldwin

No one is to blame for how you feel. Dismissing and pushing down on emotion or experience does not constitute forgiveness.

1. Spiritual 2. Self-Love 3. Healing 4. Forgiveness
I. Cat Baldwin, 1958 II. Metaphysical III. Forgiveness IV. Title

Library of Congress Catalog Card Number: 2021934783
ISBN: 9781950608027

Cover Art and Layout: Victoria Cooper Art
Book set in: Times New Roman and Book Antiqua
Book Design: Summer Garr
Published by:

OZARK
MOUNTAIN
PUBLISHING

PO Box 754, Huntsville, AR 72740
800-935-0045 or 479-738-2348; fax 479-738-2448
WWW.OZARKMT.COM

Printed in the United States of America

Contents

With Abundant Love, Joy, and Peace

To everyone throughout this lifetime who created experiences "for" me, providing the opportunity for lessons, expansion of my heart space, growth, and forgiveness. I thank you.

***

To every patient, student, and member of the spiritual community at the Wellness Sanctuary Spiritual Teaching and Healing Center and Chios Energy Healing Certification Programs, I acknowledge and honor your courage and commitment to step into your Higher Lightworker Selves. You touch, move, and inspire me every day of my life. I thank you.

***

To my son, my heart and love, who daily teaches me unconditional love, patience, acceptance, and allowing. I thank you.

***

First and always, my Source, Archangel Metatron, Archangels Michael, Gabriel, and Raphael, Anubis, Mother Mary, Mary Magdalene, Yeshua, the Galactic Council, and all Ascended Masters, ancestors, and Spirit Guides who assist me at every moment. We have waited aeons for this time. I am honored to co-create the New Earth with you all at my side with no fear, only love. I thank you.

***

To you, the reader, who knows deep within you that you are so much more and there is so much more. As you experience the power of forgiveness for yourself and all others, may you fearlessly know and be your infinite Divinity, power, and light. I thank you.

Introduction

Being in practice for over twenty years as a lightworker, healer, teacher, life/soul and spiritual advisor and channel, I have had the profound privilege of preparing souls to awaken to their True/Higher Selves in preparation for "The Shift" to fourth- and fifth-dimensional living. The preparation is both personal and for the benefit of society as well. I am humbled by this Mission at this time on planet Earth as I have been waiting and preparing for it for many lifetimes (1,100 to my knowledge).

I am the facilitator for Source through the Teachers of Light, Archangel Metatron, Mother Mary, Mary Magdalene, and Yeshua to name a few of a virtual football field filled with the light and love of these higher beings and Archangels. They are my loves, my family, my heart, and my very essence. We are co-creators of the New Earth and the ascension of Mother Earth and humanity as are all of you.

In complete surrender, my life is committed to this Mission, and every step of the way, I am guided to what each individual needs for healing and what the community needs as a whole for growth, myself included.

It is April 11, 2020, as I complete this book. Our lives have experienced a complete upheaval by the appearance of the coronavirus. This is one of the biggest blessings we are ever to receive as humanity as this is the beginning of the creation of the New Golden Age. Great darkness is being removed at this time which has held this planet and its people hostage for thousands of years.

We have been placed on lockdown as a country and are experiencing the pain of all global citizens in navigating this time. There is great opportunity and grace being given. The removal from outside distractions has provided an opportunity to go deep within through quiet introspection. Are we creating new priorities? Are we realizing how little we actually do need materially to be safe and provided for? Have we realized that we are working for companies that are void of integrity and do not value us or anyone for that matter?

Are we in our heart space with gratitude for all that is occurring no matter what? Are we embracing the adversity as thank you or are we angry, fearful, riddled with anxiety, and unwilling to accept what is truly occurring? When given the chance, are we helping those who cannot help themselves or are we continuing to be self-serving generated by fear?

We are all awakening. There are no exceptions. We must be responsible for what has come before and be clear that we will not be returning to that as it is unsustainable for humanity and for Mother Earth. If you are resisting you are being triggered by unresolved trauma whether from childhood or throughout your life. Unresolved trauma and the emotions associated with it will be continuously brought to you in various experiences until addressed.

There is also fear associated with stepping into your True Self as many are unaware of what that looks like. All things "unfamiliar" are uncomfortable at first. It is a life of joy, peace, and freedom as it is who you truly are as I share in my first book *Divine Gifts of Healing: My Life with Spirit.*

You cannot resolve trauma and victimization without forgiveness: forgiveness of yourself first and foremost, followed by all others that you feel have done things "to" you. There is a great difference from forgiveness from your ego and forgiveness from Higher Self/Spirit.

I honor and acknowledge you for stepping in to this journey and taking on forgiveness with this work. It takes courage to be personally responsible for how your life goes. I am humbled and honored to facilitate this work with you. As you take this step, the Teachers of Light, Ascended Masters, Archangels, and Spirit Guides are cheering wildly and are right at your side.

They hold and embrace you in unconditional love as do I. Shine on!

Healing Love and Light,

Cat

Please visit me at wellnesssanctuary.net

On Facebook @ Cat Baldwin, The Wellness Sanctuary Spiritual Teaching and Healing Center and Chios Energy Healing Certification Programs

On instagram @ catbaldwinwellnesssanctuary

On meetup @WheatonWellness/

Chapter 1
Why Forgive?

"Forgiveness is not about forgetting. It is about letting go of another person's throat. Forgiveness does not create a relationship. Unless people speak the truth about what they have done and change their mind and behavior, a relationship of trust is not possible. When you forgive someone, you certainly release them from judgment, but without true change, no real relationship can be established.

"Forgiveness in no way requires that you trust the one you forgive. But should they finally confess and repent, you will discover a miracle in your own heart that allows you to reach out and begin to build a bridge of reconciliation. Forgiveness does not excuse anything. You may have to declare your forgiveness a hundred times the first and the second day, but the third day will be less and each day after, until one day you will realize that you have forgiven completely. And then one day you will pray for his/her wholeness."

—William Paul Young, *The Shack*

Blessings and welcome to "The Forgiveness Workshop from Higher Self/Spirit." This continues our conversation of growth and expansion which began in my first book *Divine Gifts of Healing: My Life with Spirit*. I am Cat Baldwin, facilitator of this coursework, owner of the Wellness Sanctuary

Spiritual Teaching and Healing Center and the Chios Energy Healing Certification Programs in Warrenville, Illinois. This is one of many courses, certification programs, and services offered to support moving into your Higher Self and your personal sovereignty. It is why I am here.

Forgiveness Workshop was created in September 2017, when guidance and a request was given to me by Spirit to provide two very important gatherings. I was asked to form a Healing Circle in nature where we could all share our intentions for ourselves, one another, and the planet. The Healing Circle at the Grotto was then co-created with Spirit.

A statue of Mother Mary is the core of the Grotto. This has nothing to do with religion but with her Divine Mother energy of peace and deep, unconditional love. It is the energy Mary exudes and represents in the Universe for all. From our first gathering, nine women committed to living life from the heart and sending healing light and energy to Mother Earth and the planet. Personal intentions were shared and supportive conversations flowed. And from this gathering, the next request was made by Spirit.

"You have not forgiven many people. They include men and women as well. You have forgiven on a human/ego level but certainly not on a Higher Self/Spirit level. Instead of asking what has someone done TO you, consider what they have done FOR you. Did they do their jobs well? What did they teach you and what was/ is the lesson? Overcome your human response of judgment, blame, and self-righteousness and embrace with unconditional love and gratitude all that has been provided."

This was certainly a communication which, to fully receive, I needed to go into my heart space, breathe and feel care, appreciation, and compassion. When this was shared with the Grotto group, "Forgiveness Workshop from Higher Self/Spirit" was created. As we addressed our trauma, Spirit assured me that they would be present to guide, answer, and clear through me facilitating Life/Spiritual Advisement, Chios Energy Healing, or further one-on-one sessions. As we continue on this healing journey through this work, know that all guidance, conversations, and healings are occurring through Spirit.

Chapter 2
Prebirth Planning

I was then guided to study prebirth planning (*Your Soul's Plan* and *Your Soul's Gift* by Robert Schwartz ... extraordinary work) and everything started to become very clear. I did understand that we reincarnate to experience and clear negative thoughtforms, patterns, and behaviors from past lives and to heal. We learn through opposites on Earth as this is a planet of duality. How can we truly experience love if we have nothing to compare it to? Ultimately, we are here to recreate the frequency of Home, which can only be achieved through complete forgiveness and unconditional love, our Higher Selves/Spirit.

We are responsible for creating everything in our lives. To live any other way would have one remain in a victim mode. This information is difficult to receive but trust me, it is truth and your path to freedom. Yes, you chose your parents and your parents chose you as well. Your "soul group" consists of many people who have reincarnated in different positions in different lifetimes with you. Many who have committed the most heinous acts in your life are your greatest teachers.

"The more profound the challenge, the more likely it was chosen before birth. One important exception, however, concerns experiences our intuition warns us to avoid. Unplanned challenges can occur when we ignore our intuitive promptings; therefore, internal 'danger signals' are to be acknowledged and honored at all times.

"When we incarnate, we have free will, and we can exercise our free will to create challenges that were not part of our pre-birth planning. The operative word is create. I believe we are the creators of everything we experience, and unplanned challenges occur when we vibrationally draw them to us because we need the wisdom they can engender. Our growth derives from the experiences themselves, regardless of whether or not we planned them. In such instances, intuition will not guide us away from what we need.

"You may find the concept of pre-birth planning, particularly the planning of painful challenges—astonishing. The more traumatic our challenges, the more difficult the concept may be. I only ask that you consider its possibility. You need not be convinced of the idea to benefit from it. You need only ask, 'What if? What if I really did plan this experience before I was born? Why might I have done that?' Simply asking these questions gives new meaning to life challenges and launches a journey of healing, forgiveness and self-discovery."

In *Your Soul's Gift*, Robert Schwartz touches upon deeply traumatic experiences such as incest, rape, and AIDS. I would like to share further direct quotes from Robert as I am in alignment with his communication and feel it's necessary to include in this work.

"As I considered the subject of incest for this book, I alternated between viewing it through the lens of the soul and the human lens. From the soul perspective, I saw once again an opportunity to offer healing, and I felt hopeful as well as humbled and honored to do this work. From the human perspective, however, I felt fear.

"How could I possibly suggest to the world, and in particular to people who have experienced incest, that something so traumatic would, or even could, be planned by the soul? If the Universe were indeed asking me to put forth this awareness, how could I do so with love and compassion? In particular, I was concerned that those who have experienced incest might feel blame, judgment, or guilt in regard to the planning of any experience. I prayed, asked for guidance, and moved forward knowing that my path would be illuminated.

"With my ultimate goal of healing, forgiveness and release, I felt that this conversation must be shared.

"Two personal shares of incest, one where the mother had agreed in pre-birth planning that she would stop the incest but she did not. This was to clear the ancestral line from continuing to repeat this behavior. The second case shared was quite different as the writer agreed in pre-birth planning for the incest to occur. She wanted to heal the world this time. Her life had to have sorrow, pain, grief and hurt in enough measure to invoke personal healing. If she had been comfortable, the impetus for personal healing would not be as great. If the hurt were not enough for personal upliftment, her contribution to the world, as a Psychotherapist specializing in Sexual Abuse would have been less passionate and significant.

"She had helped from a safe distance before in past lives, but when it became her story too, she had to get involved in a much deeper committed way. Through personal healing she knows what healing feels like. She can guide people through their pain in steadfastness and love, because she came through it herself. Thus, she can be more energetically impactful in the world. You reach more people through the healing of yourself.

"Healing yourself changes the vibrational frequency of your generational line: your past, present and future selves. Forgiveness also changes the vibration, which affects all involved. By healing yourself, you help uplift the entire planet because you are contributing love, peace, and forgiveness rather than lower vibrational emotions. Stop fighting yourself, surrender and allow. Healing will occur naturally if allowed."

Without going too deeply into these difficult life experiences, I highly recommend you read both of these books to gain a deeper understanding of the most challenging occurrences. Actual cases and people are featured. It is with my deepest love and compassion, and to not invalidate the pain of these occurrences, that I recommend these reads for healing if this is a personal experience.

Chapter 3
Nothing Is by Chance

Consider that every single person you've met in your life was there for one of these five cosmic reasons.

The Universe that we live in works in mysterious ways. There is chaos in the complexities of its functioning and yet everything is balanced.

It can be rightly said that nothing in this Universe happens by chance.

Even the most insignificant incidents happen as planned and serve a greater purpose. Everything that happens is a manifestation of the cosmos.

Our journey through life is not entirely a smooth ride. There are ups and downs. Some roads are rough and others are not.

Life is a mystery where all experiences hold equal importance and value. We are lucky that the Universe keeps track of our journey.

Throughout this journey, we meet different people who play different roles and serve different purposes.

Some teach us certain life lessons, while others do not leave a lasting impact on us.

Some people are meant to stay with us forever, while others are not. But even the people we meet are not by chance!

These are the five types of cosmic connections that we are likely to encounter on our journey:

1. Those meant to awaken us

There are times in our lives when we encounter people who are agents of change. They walk into our lives to directly or indirectly initiate some change.

Their very presence makes us aware that we cannot move forward in life unless we effect certain changes. The universe has its ways of working such things out.

These people will awaken your inner dormant potential that would have stayed asleep if you remained stuck.

2. Those who remind us

Sometimes in life we come across people who stop by only to remind us of our goals.

The only purpose of such interactions is to help us remain focused on our path in life.

These people remind us of who we are and what we truly wanted since the beginning.

3. Those who help us grow

Some people help us grow as a person. They stand by us as a guide in our journey through life. They might hurt us or invite us

on an adventure to face a challenge.
They show us our way when we seem to be unaware of the right path. They teach us things that we are unable to learn by ourselves.
These people stretch us in order to grow.

4. <u>Those who hold space for us</u>

Some people play such insignificant roles in our lives that we do not even remember their names. These are mostly people we meet at the subway or on the roads or at a coffee house.

They are simply meant to hold a space for us. They are usually the people we make small talk with and have no connection beyond that.

These people are your fellow companions that greet you on your journey, or even personal soul fans that unconsciously cheer for the good in you!

5. <u>Those who stay</u>

There are only a few people who will stick by us forever. These people are rare to find but certainly are the most precious ones.

They are our close friends and our immediate family. Most of them are members of our soul group, some of them might even be our soulmates.

These people are your partners that share the same or a really similar mission.

But when the time is right, the Universe will send us that one person who is meant to be with us forever. This person is another group separate from all others.

The presence of this person makes everything feel better. We just need to be patient in our attempts at finding them. But once we find them, they are meant to stay.

Please, have compassion and gratitude, and sometimes you must find that forgiveness within yourself. If nothing is by chance, it is all for your highest and greatest good. Embrace all experiences with love, gratitude, and thankfulness.

Chapter 4
Let's Get Started

We started with creating our list of people who we feel needed our forgiveness. An interesting question came up shortly after the second class. How many of us put "Self" on this list and if we did, where was it placed? Two of us, including me, did not even have self on the list!! For several of the group, self was last on the list. Just as in self-love, you certainly cannot forgive on the Higher Self/Spirit level without forgiving yourself.

From day one, each of us struggled with this technique as radiating appreciation, care, and compassion for OURSELVES does not come easily to us. We are taught from childhood to sacrifice our needs and place the needs of others first, much to our detriment. "Don't be selfish." This programming has caused a great deal of harm for many. A very powerful book that I discovered at an early age was *You Can Heal Your Life* by Louise Hay. I have worked with my patients/students in this book for nearly fifteen years. Unless you can generate self-love it will be next to impossible to generate self-compassion or self-forgiveness. Everyone is diligently working from the concepts of this book.

When generating self-love, you are no longer using the past to keep you victimized. If you're unwilling to take responsibility for what you've created by agreement, you will remain victimized and will continue to blame others and outside factors for what is or has occurred. Taking responsibility frees you from the past, empowering you to create something new.

When you are unwilling to forgive, that is your ego currently running the show! Ego was created for survival and protection. My experience is, the more deeply emotionally traumatized you have been, the more rooted in ego and survival you are. "Oh, it's their fault. They are wrong ... blah, blah, blah." When you find yourself in this place as we all do, and your ego rears its ugly head and wants to do its will in its domain, say out loud, "Yeah, I get that. But this is the thing. I created you, ego, as eventually something I'm going to wake up out of. I unravel, scoop you up, and put you back in my heart space with love. It's not about the fear, it's about the love."

Just know this in your deepest heart space that anything that causes separation is from the ego, not from Spirit, which is who you really are. You are Spirit in a physical body, not a physical body trying to be spiritual. We are all one energy.

A human being is a meaning-making machine. Something happens and we make it mean something. It's just what happened and that's just what's so. Don't get me wrong. I'm very clear when deep emotional trauma and pain have occurred that this can certainly cause scarring and fear, particularly if you were violated as a defenseless child with no voice or power. Taking back your power allows you to come from a space of responsibility where you will no longer tolerate behaviors or occurrences that do not directly serve your highest good. This is where forgiveness of self and others is crucial to the healing process.

The other key aspect brought to my attention is to fully release the emotion associated with that person. That experience must be brought to the surface, felt deeply, and released. You will know when you've succeeded when you can talk about a person or occurrence and no longer be emotionally activated. If you are still feeling anger, sadness, injustice, fear instead of joy and love, there is more work to do! You will continually be activated by others/experiences until that emotion/thoughtform is released. Otherwise, that person has taken up residence in your head, rent free!! I acknowledge and honor each of you for taking on the challenge of being here. These are not easy choices to make. Remember that each and every person did these things out of love for you and your growth.

Truly be with the fact that all that occurs is in Divine Order, that it is for your highest and greatest good, and that you created all of it. To live in Spirit, who you truly are, is to surrender each day, requesting divine guidance, and being at peace with ALL that occurs ... EVERYTHING. If living in this state of energy, is there really anything to forgive?

This is the sharing of actual breakthroughs and healings that have occurred in Forgiveness Workshop. No one escapes "the process" of growth and expansion to your Higher Self. It's impossible to not be who you truly are, Spirit in a physical body. It is your eternal self. Your ego will fight with all its might to stay in control, filling your mind with fear, lies, and ingrained programming from this and many lifetimes. Just know this, the more you resist, the more it persists.

But remember, the ego was created for the purpose of protection, oftentimes during very difficult and abusive childhoods. Due to lifetime experiences, we have conversations programmed that run in our background. "You're not safe." "Be careful, you cannot trust anyone." "You will never amount to anything." "You're ugly, stupid, and fat" … etc., etc., etc. … right?

Don't know about you but what certainly ran in my background for many years was "Nothing I do is ever good enough. I will never be good enough." You then think if you act like other people, you are okay. Or my biggest misperception throughout most of my life was how amazing and incredible someone was. Needless to say, as time went on, they were not. My ego, lack of self-love, lack of self-respect, and insecurity were running my life.

How about you? The ego sweeps in and continues reinforcing these conversations. Looking at the people connected to them, it's human nature to blame, have true feelings of deep resentment, anger, and hatred. In order to "survive" many of us were taught to stuff our feelings, buck up, and be strong, not knowing that these occurrences in our lives left deep emotional scars.

This Workshop will support you in moving out of the ego's control and into your Higher Self/ Spirit. One of the most powerful ways to do this is through forgiveness. When the ego chimes in with the chatter, and trust me it will throughout this process, the response is simple. Say out loud or to yourself, "Yes, I get that and thank you for sharing. That's not my truth any longer. Thank you for all you have provided. My soul and my heart space are expanding. I scoop you up and return you to Source with love. No fear, only love."

Let us begin with a heart-based meditation from the Heart Math Institute, utilized before Workshop and throughout your day for three to five minutes, whenever possible.

Step 1. Focus your attention in the area of the heart. Imagine your breath is flowing in and out of your heart or chest area, breathing a little slower and deeper than usual.

Step 2. Activate and sustain a regenerative feeling such as appreciation, care, or compassion.

Step 3. Radiate that renewing feeling to yourself and others.

One of the biggest benefits of learning to follow your heart's promptings will be the ability to bring your mental and emotional faculties into greater alignment with your true self.

My first question is, did you send compassion, appreciation, and care to yourself? And if not, why not? Next conversation, "No one is to blame for how you feel." I can hear the ego's response to that! I would like you to consider what it would be like to not blame people, places, and things for how you feel. It would actually mean that YOU are responsible for how things go. Feeling empowered yet? If not, you are committed to being a victim, which again is ego rearing its ugly head.

I would also like to offer an invaluable option in forgiving that is connecting to your Higher Heart (as written by Stasia Bliss):

"Nestled between the heart and the throat sits an often unrecognized energy center which brings the consciousness and signatures of these two area's chakras together in a beautiful, harmonious, powerful way. Known by many as the 'High Heart' or 'Chakra 4.5' this chakra is all about living your personal truth and doing so with passion and conviction.

"Anahata Chakra in the chest helps us tune into unconditional love and healing energy which, when grounded into the lower chakras, stimulates a powerful volt of energy, making its way for the throat center. Passing by the thymus gland, the body's main immune gland, the high-heart center takes the heart chakra's energy and draws down the clarity of the throat into a throbbing, centering, deep heart knowing which gives you the sense that you have purpose which can actually make an impact on the world.

"This can be done by using tapping, gently over the sternum/thymus area with the fingertips, thereby stimulating this vital center and helping to reset the body's immune system. The Thymus Chakra is the seat of compassion, empathy, joy, peace, serenity, patience, balanced emotions and unconditional love for those that are close to you."

One of the important qualities this chakra is responsible for is *forgiveness*. This is a powerful emotion ... and one that many of you may find difficult to deal with. Many of you have been holding on to negative energy and have been unable to forgive others. You may have carried this with you for many years. By activating the Higher Heart chakra, you may find that you are able to release and let go of these feelings. If you are unfamiliar with chakras, please purchase my first book *Divine Gifts of Healing: My Life with Spirit*, which contains an extensive chakra education.

Let's move on to what I call "The Forgiveness Formula" questions as addressed through Higher/ Self and Spirit.

1. Instead of asking what has someone done TO you, consider what they have done FOR you.
2. Did they do their jobs well?
3. What did they teach you and what was/is the lesson?
4. Overcome your human response of judgment, blame, and self-righteousness

and embrace with unconditional love and gratitude all that has been provided for you.

You can certainly have quite the ego/human response to these questions. Particularly the last line of having unconditional love and gratitude for all that has been provided for you. Are you kidding me right now? That is how impactful this work is to changing your very heart and life experiences from this point forward.

Change is up to you. Embrace your Higher Self/Spirit or remain in ego, pain, blame, and limitation. We are no longer children who had no voice or no power. We create boundaries of what is acceptable and unacceptable as well. Let's grab your workbook or notebook and get started!

Chapter 5
Forgiveness List

List everyone who you feel needs forgiveness and please write the emotion which this person evokes in you. Do not spare anyone (laughs). Pick the top five people that had the greatest impact on you and along with the emotions, please answer "The Forgiveness Formula" questions as thoroughly as possible. You may then move on with your list of people and the emotions associated with each. If you feel the need to really dig into each person and write an extensive experience using "The Forgiveness Formula" questions then please do so.

I have a list that encompassed 60 people, and I have seen lists that encompass over 150. The point of this is not to point fingers or blame, it is to heal from a higher perspective than your ego, from your Higher Self, and truly release victimization and embrace growth and expansion.

Who do you feel is the most important person to forgive first and foremost? While so many of us have deep wounded inner children (that's an entire Workshop in and of itself, which we are currently embarking on) and we may feel that our parents need our forgiveness first, while it is imperative, they are not the most important. YOU are.

The following is my letter of self-forgiveness.

I choose to forgive myself for allowing manipulation and inauthenticity to fool me throughout my life. To forgive that I always looked at others as more or better than me based on unexplained events at the age of four, when my father abandoned his family. I lost sight of my Divinity giving unconditional love without boundaries. To forgive myself for poor choices in relationships, but to have gratitude and clarity that they all occurred for my growth, lessons, and divine plan.

I have taught myself to stand in my power. To re-member that I am Spirit in a physical body having a human experience with the only limitations being self-imposed. To trust and listen to my own inner knowing as it is the only guidance that I need along with co-creation and relationship with my Archangels, Ascended Masters, ancestors, and Spirit Guides.

I have taught myself to stand in what I know to be my truth, my word, with integrity. To be the example of what I am requesting of others. I have learned that negative attention is not love, nor is it good attention. Sex is not love, nor are words which are not followed up by action.

I have learned that I am so much more than my looks and my physical body. They are merely the vessel which I have chosen to house my spirit in this lifetime. Unconditional love and respect come from me for myself first. Then and only then can it be given to others and received by me from others.

I am looking for what my lessons were learning through opposites. Love unconditionally but with boundaries of self-care, self-respect, and self-love. I am a Spiritual Warrior in this lifetime, no weapons, only love. But love that is pure, not fear based, for manipulative personal ego gains or to complete someone's personal agenda.

Our energy and sexuality are sacred to be used for healing, growth, and expansion. When my true partner and I are brought together, we will share in this sacred ritual to continue to accelerate the ascension process together. We will be more powerful together than we are apart in the commitment of the highest good for ourselves and all people on the planet.

I have learned that trust and loyalty are not given, they are earned. That noble souls will continue to be in my life as they also have my highest good at heart. Source (Supreme Creator) is my provider. I am safe in my Divinity and inner knowing that I am a spark of Source, a part of universal Cosmic energy and all that is and the only thing it is, is love.

The world will occur as I choose to see it. We are all on the path to ultimately remember HOME and to live here to create the vibration of HOME on this planet.

I trust and surrender that all that occurs in each and every present moment is divine and for my highest and greatest good. I forgive myself for giving away my power but know that everything that has occurred has brought me to where and who I am today and for honoring others and not honoring myself first. I forgive myself for not ensuring that my needs were met first and no need for explanation when I do so. I am never alone, and therefore I am never lonely. I will choose and co-create my life here and will accomplish what I came here to do.

Where did that come from? It was created after looking at each person on my list, writing the feelings which they invoked in me, taking responsibility for it, and looking at what was done for me, not to me. If I may share some examples with you?

I addressed my parents next as I feel they had the greatest impact on my life. My father left when I was four; my mother spent the remainder of her life dealing with the impact of that through her own dysfunction as best as she possibly could. They are both now deceased.

Mom
Emotions Associated Fear, Mistrust, Negativity, Criticism, Judgment

Mom made me strong and responsible but unfortunately over responsible to my self-detriment and the benefit of others. The world is not harsh, unloving, brutal, and difficult. I am clear this is how it occurred for her. Life is not about just surviving your situation. The world will occur the way I choose to see it as will people.

Money, and people with a lot of it, are not snobs or evil, nor do they have the power to make me "less than" as this does not determine value.

Her life inside the box with concern of outside appearances and what others think created a rebelliousness within me not to be put in that box. I would not live my life in familial expectations and social agreement. I questioned everything I was being told and was ultimately on a quest for my own truth due to her limitations. Mom taught me love is actions, not words.

Through her life experience, betrayed by my father and abused by an alcoholic second husband, she showed me that being safe and secure is not about a house in the suburbs and money in the bank. Being safe can only occur within me, my value, self-love, and self-respect. I am perfect, whole, and complete at every moment and always safe.

She did the best with what she had based on her deep inner-child emotional wounds that were never addressed or healed. Her pushing—which occurred for me as "never good enough"—was how she felt about herself. She wanted so much more for me to be my very best.

This is what has created who I am today. I sought healing at the age of thirteen and continue to this day, providing the same for others. I am a person of integrity, compassion, and empathy open to allow love, gratitude, and abundance into my life. Thank you, Mom, for all you provided.

Dad

Emotions Associated with Abandonment, Survival, Egocentricity

My father wanted me to be a boy. Understand, we feel this in utero, even before birth. I was a tomboy through high school until I sought healing. I am wanted, loved, feminine, and divine and I am good enough. My father left his family for another woman when I was four. The actions and choices of others, wherever they are on their journey, is not a direct reflection, nor any reflection of who I am or my personal value, nor is it my responsibility.

An insatiable need for attention and self-aggrandizement truly reflected the open inner-child wound of lack of love from his own parents. Take personal responsibility for the choices you make and the impact they have on others. Be in communication about those choices as a child does not understand that they are not responsible.

When he stepped back into my life after thirty-five years, he then took credit that his genetics were responsible for what an amazing human being I had become. Genetics do not determine if someone is a "father" or "mother." Nor does it determine who is "family" in your life. Care, nurturing, and availability determine the level of contribution and impact someone has in your life. Do not take credit for anything you have not personally had a contribution to the direct outcome to alleviate your guilt and lack of contribution.

My father taught me to accept and take responsibility for the harm I may have done, clean it up, and commit to it not occurring again. I am committed to contribution and the greatness of others consistently. Thank you, Dad, for all you provided.

Are you getting the idea here? The key is to really sit with this emotion, allow it to come to the surface, breathe deeply, and see it release. Visualize the emotion in words, fill with white light, and transmute them to the words light and love. And again, when these emotions get re-activated/triggered by other occurrences in your life, these relationships may have been the point of origin. The emotion/thoughtform has not been fully released from the programming or experience. Get in touch with the emotion and do it again. Consistent Chios Energy Healing Sessions to clear these layers as they are exposed is recommended whether with me personally at my facility or via distance healing.

Many of these emotions are being activated by our Wounded Inner Child. You will get in touch with these emotions as you work through your family. The Wounded Inner Child will continually poke at your stomach/digestion in an attempt to get your attention. As you do this work, please get in touch with her/him by placing your hand on your stomach, gently rubbing and visualizing yourself as a child. Bend down so you are eye to eye and embrace her/him. "You are amazing and I am so happy you are here. You are perfect, whole, and complete at every moment. You are safe and I will protect you. I love you unconditionally and I will never leave you. I hear you and acknowledge your feelings and we will work through this together." Please visualize big hugs and kisses between you. You have become your inner child's parent.

For many decades, some lightworkers (including myself) had the mission of clearing/ healing the mass consciousness. If you have experienced an intense emotion come over you for no apparent reason whatsoever, this is what is occurring. Please say out loud, "May all who are feeling _____ (insert the emotion you are feeling) be healed, blessed, and transformed."

With billions of people on the planet, you can imagine the huge undertaking this was. I have recently been informed by Spirit that we are no longer responsible for "Clean-up in Aisle 7." The energy and vibration of the planet has been raised and cleared for everyone to access healing and live into their Higher Self.

Chapter 6
Challenges

When we came together weekly, sharing would encompass a thought/emotion from the list and the occurrence(s) associated with it or in daily life, something was triggered that activated emotions uncleared.

One participant had a narcissistic husband and two daughters who treated her horrendously. When empowered, a divorce occurred. With both daughters being adults, and not living with her, it was her choice as to whether she was going to have a relationship with them. Yes, CHOOSING to have a relationship is not determined by family. Having blood lineage does not give anyone permission to mistreat or disrespect you.

When she chose to respect herself and sever communication, the repair work began. As she respected herself and created boundaries, respect was given to her. When a daughter becomes abusive in any way, there is no response given. Consider looking at your wife, husband, mother, father, etc., as a person, without the societal title that has been imposed. With this title also comes expectations of behaviors, language, and situations. If they were viewed as a person, would you like them or even allow them in your life? What emotions would be expressed in this situation? Pain, hurt, anger, rage?

Expectation creates an attachment to an outcome that ultimately leads to disappointment. The only expectation you may consider having is what's acceptable to you in how you want to be treated. What are your boundaries?

The disrespect and abuse were tolerated for many years due to this experience as a child. "I'm not good enough" ran in the background for decades, attracting a family that perpetuated this belief. When healing began and emotion/ thoughtforms were addressed, this way of being was no longer tolerated from family, nor was it believed. A new, more powerful way of being was created due to what was done "for" this person, not "to" this person. This created life-changing lessons of self-love, self-respect, and self-forgiveness. Thank you!

Can you imagine thinking for forty years that you were the cause of your grandmother's death? As a teenager expressing growing independence, one of the Workshop participants recalls her grandmother, in front of a large group of people, saying, "This is my baby, everyone." With indignation she stormed off, saying, "I'm not a baby, Grandma." Several weeks later her grandmother passed away and she felt it was because of what she said to her. Doing her Workshop questions and in meditation, there was a recalled memory of Grandma saying to her, "I know you're not a baby anymore. It's okay." Apologies were exchanged and all was well. She had completely forgotten this.

The healing work we were doing and the space we were providing allowed connection to a memory that previously had not been recalled. This occurred through self-forgiveness work and no longer carrying the burden of being a selfish, mean person. It was the typical response of a teenager who didn't love her grandma any less but was asserting her growth and independence … all healthy. Thank you!

Being in practice for twenty years, it has been my experience that physical manifestation of dis-ease or illness, discomfort of any sort is the manifestation of emotional trauma/harm that has never been cleared from the body. Something occurs, we make it mean something based on experience, societal or familial agreement, and the body responds.

A participant with consistent acid reflux, indigestion, and digestive issues had endured severe abuse as a child. Indigestion is gut-level fear, dread, and anxiety, griping and grunting. The inner child lives in your solar plexus chakra (your stomach). When the inner child continues to be invalidated by not addressing and healing past issues, it will manifest out physically. Your body is talking. Are you listening? This participant felt the need to "fix" everything and ensure everyone was happy but was made to feel she was in the way. It was a hypervigilant way of controlling the environment to ensure her safety.

This participant's husband was begrudgingly working on a home project that he chose to do.

She was not feeling well but said she would help. She went to lay down and he called her to help. He was measuring but never said anything out loud. He then asked her what the measurements were. She felt like a child again, not good enough, powerless, and trying to make things better by being kind. What's the lesson?

Forgive herself for compromising her well-being. Forgive him for being rude and crass. This was his choice in his way of being. He would not share what or why he was being this way. Instead, he chose to be short with her, which activated her childhood memory of being powerless, never good enough, and responsible for "fixing" things. Also deeply ingrained, "This must be my fault."

What did he do for her? By activating this feeling, he allowed her to choose whether she was going to participate with him by helping. It empowered her to choose not to be disrespected by walking away and advising him that she was available to help if he would like to communicate the reason for his behavior and change it toward her. Bringing up this emotion from childhood is a thank-you to Spirit and her husband as it has given her an opportunity to change the outcome to one where she has boundaries and is empowered.

Did he do his job well? Absolutely and what did she get out of it? That her husband's behavior is his choice. Even if he's upset, but unwilling to communicate, she's not obligated to be disrespected and mistreated. She's not responsible for fixing anything. This is for him to resolve.

She has always been the "fixer" for people,

a learned behavior from childhood to make a difficult tense environment more manageable. When you are a "fixer," you enable others to not do their work or be responsible for their behavior. You are also saying in a subconscious way that they are not capable of managing and healing themselves or their life.

The emotion attached to this was frustration and anger. We sit with this, feel and allow it to come to the surface, breathe and transmute it with love and light. Embrace with gratitude the lessons that have been provided. Thank you.

Chapter 7
Barriers to Heart-Based Connection/Consciousness

If you resist forgiving with your entire being, you are not coming from your heart. Your need to blame other persons, places, or things is a deeply ingrained programming from society and sometimes dysfunctional families, which is a familiar, comfortable way of being. Choosing to do so will block intimacy and closeness that is ultimately what we all need and want. Due to past experiences of hurt, violation, or rejection we can be fearful of allowing ourselves to be vulnerable. Some deal with this by having to control every aspect of their existence, limiting all possibility of peace, joy, the abundance of the Universe, and the serendipity of life to occur.

This limits closeness, trust, and relationship. Are you committed to being "right" no matter what? And if so, what is that costing you? Know this, it's my experience in twenty years of practice, that when one refuses to forgive, clear and open the heart space, heart disease eventually follows.

Here are some of the things that impact a true heart-based connection.

1. <u>Victim vs. Empowerment</u> Take responsibility and create clear boundaries.
2. <u>Blame vs. Responsibility</u> (for feelings and their impact on you) Remember, no one is to blame for how you feel. Communicate how something occurs for you but you are being triggered and the issue needs to be addressed.
3. <u>Story vs. Just Being with What's So</u> A human being is a meaning-making machine. Something happens and we make it mean something. Be with what has occurred with no story around it and communicate what is not working for you.
4. <u>Separation vs. Oneness</u> Separation, judgment, blame, and finger pointing are all ego based. Create boundaries and if it just isn't working for you this may not be a relationship or person who belongs in your life. Release what is no longer for your highest good. We are all one universal energy. Judgment of others is fear based. What really underlies judgment is "I'm not good enough."
5. <u>Vibration of Your Thoughtforms</u> Negative thoughts can decrease your vibrational frequency. The human body vibrates at an average of 68 mHz. Every negative emotion, thoughtform, and communication decreases that frequency. Death occurs when the body is at 25 mHz. Positive thoughts and emotions raise your frequency by 10 mHz as does ten minutes of meditation. Will you give away your

power to someone or something? Your choice.

6. <u>Expectations/Attachment to an Outcome</u> Having an expectation and specific attachment to an outcome from someone or something ultimately leads to disappointment. No one has any right to claim to "know" what someone will do, what they will say, or how they will react.

7. <u>Lack of Self-Love</u> Without self-love, you cannot forgive. Childhood emotional trauma and life experiences will dictate what is running in your background. "I'm not good enough." "I'm stupid." Without self-love, we look outside ourselves for validation, fulfillment, emotional needs, and more. All you need is inside of you to achieve "emotional independence." This means looking to oneself as the primary source of one's well-being. When that is healed, you can then clearly see and forgive what others have done "for" you. Without healing, that's a no-win situation for everyone.

Please consider the following excerpt from *The Jeshua Channelings: Christ Consciousness in a New Era* by Pamela Kribbe. These are the channelings of the teachings of Jeshua Ben Joseph, whom you may know as Jesus.

35

"When you take a closer look at your own roles or identities, you soon notice there have been painful, even traumatic experiences in your past, which still 'stick to you.' You seem unable to let them go. They have become like a 'second skin,' skin instead of a mere garment.

"Those are the difficult elements in your past, the pieces that now keep you from truly living and enjoying life. You have identified so much with these parts, that you think you are them. Because of this you feel you are a victim and you draw negative conclusion from this about life. But these conclusions do not hold for life as such; they just hold for the traumatized parts in your soul consciousness.

"It is these parts that need healing now. You do so by entering the past again, but with a consciousness that is more loving and wise than you ever had before. In the second stage of the transformation process from ego to heart, you heal episodes from the past by encircling them with your present consciousness. Through reexperiencing them in the present, from a heart centered focus, you will let go of the traumatic parts of the past.

"Trauma occurs when you experience a great loss or pain or evil and you cannot understand why it happens. You have all experienced trauma in many of your lives. In fact, the soul's consciousness during the ego stage is traumatized from the outset: there is the loss of Oneness or Home that it remembers and does not understand.

"When you go back to the original traumatic

event through imagination and you encircle it with the consciousness of the heart, you are changing your original response to the event. You change it from horror and disbelief, to simply taking note of what happens. In the regression, you simply take note of what happened and this very act creates room for understanding, room for a spiritual understanding of what actually took place in this event. When this room is present, you are becoming master of your reality again. You are now able to come to an acceptance of the whole episode, since you understand from the heart that there is meaning and purpose to everything that happens.

"You can sense from the heart that there is an element of free choice present in everything that occurs, and so you grow towards an acceptance of your own responsibility for the event. When you accept your own responsibility, you are free to move on."

Beautifully said and thank you, Jeshua. Certainly gives better understanding of why we start Workshop with heart-based meditation. You are here to heal yourself and to step into your Christed Energy. This can only occur through heart-consciousness.

Is your ego shouting at the moment (laughs)? Please just be with the communication from your heart space and breathe. Are you in your workbook yet? Have you begun the process? If not, why not?

Chapter 8
Responsibility

When you are fully aware that the man you have been with for four years and now live with has no intention of getting married, is it in your best interest to stay in a relationship where you want to be married? Do you think you are going to change his mind? Is that a healthy expectation to have?

The space that you are sharing does not have your name on the lease. Would you be here? An argument ensues about being included on the lease and possibly purchasing a home together. The woman asks, "Well, why not just get married?" He blows up and throws her out with no concern for her well-being or where she will go. Would you return to this situation?

This is a man who gave everything away to his ex-wife in their divorce. He sees his daughter, which the ex-wife shares time with as well, but he will not consider any activities as a "family" for fear that he will not be allowed to see his daughter. Sounds to me like a man who is fully aware that he has total control of all aspects of this "relationship."

This participant certainly created this situation.

Taking full responsibility moves you from victim to empowerment. Forgiveness of self certainly was the first point to consider. Fear compromises our self-love and self-respect to stay with someone who may not be what's best for us. The fear that we may be alone is not a reason to remain in a relationship as ultimately it is healthier to be alone. As with most circumstances, these deep-seated insecurities were generated in childhood trauma.

When sitting in heart-based meditation and tackling the forgiveness questions, emotions are brought to the surface associated with parental divorce, abandonment, and ignored sexual abuse. What was done "for" her was being put in a situation where her fear of abandonment was activated and she was forced to look at her situation and choose to become independent, providing for herself. Your security lies within you, not outside of yourself.

Lessons of emotional and individual independence brought her back to a place of personal responsibility and not victimhood. Ego can certainly choose to see him as selfish, controlling, insecure, and defensive. Higher Self/ Spirit sees him as the catalyst for personal growth and independence, self-love, and self-respect generated by our participant. Thank you.

Constant abuse and bullying throughout childhood create self-doubt and very low self-esteem. Our next participant was in a pet communication class as, yes, she has the ability to connect to animals to address their specific needs and concerns.

During class, a woman whose pet she was reading kept shaking her head and saying, "No, you're not correct." Taking this as truth, our participant shut down and would not read any longer, telling herself that she couldn't do this. "You're not good enough" and "Who are you kidding?" were running in her head. This had occurred during Energy Healing sessions she had performed as well.

Of course, these conversations running in her background were left unaddressed well into adulthood. Our participant was actually, unconsciously of course, manifesting these situations to validate what she had been told her entire life. Yes, we all do this. Your thoughts are this powerful.

Just a side note here, those of us who are healers/intuitives/channelers have the responsibility of delivering the message from Spirit. How it's received is not our responsibility as quite often ego will interfere and your patient/client will not be in a state of mind to accept responsibility for your communication.

This "bad" and "wrong" state of mind created and attracted a life filled with emotional and verbal abuse. This "abuse me/hiding energy" had stopped her from pursuing all of her gifts, hopes, and dreams. Resisting the work that needs to be done comes from ego and a false sense of safety by hiding or shutting down. The ego, attempting to protect itself, gives a false sense of others being the cause—blaming.

She had deep pain, resentment, and anger

toward her brother and others, which left unreleased through emotionally getting in touch with it and forgiving from Higher Self/Spirit, will run the show her entire life. We release to create something new. Self-forgiveness was addressed first and foremost for allowing and using other people's behaviors toward her to justify her fear, exhaustion, and hiding. Forgiving herself empowers her to no longer allow such behaviors and no longer use them as an excuse to not getting what she truly wants out of her life.

She began to disassemble this by writing a letter to her brother who had sexually abused her as a child. When her brother passed on, as much as she said she forgave him, her energy was very angry. She was angry at all of her siblings for acting like it never happened and putting her in uncomfortable situations as an adult where she was exposed to her brother.

She struggled her entire life with why. I channeled communication from her brother/ abuser. He was told by his friend, whose father was a pedophile, that what he did was normal behavior and what men do in a family. His friend was abused and had abused her brother thus he did so with her. He had so much shame around this that he couldn't look her in the face. He was sexually dysfunctional his entire life (used women) and manifested cancer in his deep self-loathing, which ultimately took his life. His punishment for his actions was self-induced for the remainder of his life after someone told him it was wrong and unacceptable.

She has forgiven herself for allowing his

dysfunctional behavior to determine her self-worth, timidity, anxiety, fear, and in attracting abusive relationships. She has finally forgiven him and sees clearly what his actions "moved" her to do in the healing of her life.

This has created a very deep compassion and nonjudgmental way of being in all of her relationships. She is called to advocate for proper treatment of animals, Mother Earth, and the environment. Do you think her experiences have shaped her ultimate purpose? Thank you for all that has been provided.

During actual Workshop (Divine timing in action), a text was received accusing one of our participants of not making any effort to have a relationship with her immediate family. SHE (the accuser) had just spent time with her mother's side of the family, judging and assuming she knows the level of involvement or even has any business commenting about it with a superior attitude and tone.

Our participant was very tempted to be enrolled in this conversation by being defensive. We took a deep breath and asked her, "What's your daughter teaching you at this moment?" "What is she doing 'for' you? What's the lesson and the forgiveness?"

The lesson is self-love, self-respect, standing in her power, and knowing she's a good person, mother, and family member. If she defends herself, or feels she has to defend herself, she is agreeing with what she's being accused of! Having to defend gives your power away to the other person as you're getting enrolled in the back-and-forth volley. That's from ego, not your Higher Self/Spirit. There's nothing to defend. The emotions of hurt and frustration were brought to the surface, felt, and released. Thank you.

Our next participant was given an inadequate pay raise and bonus. When assessing the work situation, the owner gives out whatever he chooses based on how he feels about someone at the time, not on work responsibilities and performance.

This immediately triggered her feelings of "not good enough." By valuing herself and standing in her power, she created a list of all of her responsibilities to present to him for his knowledge. We also uncovered that she had in the past been way too emotionally invested. She had become his "therapist and sounding board" which interfered with her completing her responsibilities. She had been at his beck and call.

We started to address this as her lack of self-confidence and insecurity of self from childhood issues. This is how she controlled and managed her space and safety instead of standing on her merits for what a great job she did in her position. His lack of compensation was because she detached emotionally and no longer provided "therapist" support. Your place of employment is NOT the place where you are emotionally invested. Your home, yourself, and your partner is your investment space.

He was using this "comfort" and emotional attachment to control her self-image by restricting compensation which should have been earned through performance. A strong lesson that compensation in the workplace is not as important as standing in your power and self-respect of knowing you are doing a great job.

What a great lesson he taught her. She was initially angry but released, stood in her power, is amazing at her job, and is slowly gaining his respect. Thank you.

Chapter 9
Stepping into 2020

As this may seem like we are going off track in our forgiveness conversation, I felt it necessary to share. I am writing this book in the fall/ winter months of 2019 and huge earthly energy changes have been occurring since 2012. These changes are in support of your personal growth and transformation in creating a life of love, peace, contribution, and empowerment as that is who You are. YOU are love and light, a spark of the Divine. Please continue and you will see the purpose of the validity of this side road. 12:12 refers to a full moon occurring with the following of the new moon and winter solstice.

♀ 12:12 vibrates on a healing frequency; therefore, we may notice past wounds have been surfacing so they can be cleared and healed. We are going to be transcending the energy of the past ten years so that we leave the decade feeling healthier, stronger, more empowered, resilient, ready for new beginnings, and not afraid to let go of those familiar but harmful and limiting energies.

We are about to enter an extremely intense ten-day energy portal, starting on 12-12 and ending 12-21, that will cleanse debilitating toxins from our lives. This includes unhealthy habits, conditioned behaviors, outdated beliefs, and irrational fear-based thoughts and feelings that diminish our energy and leave us feeling irritable, anxious, and burnt-out.

Any ties that energetically bind us to people or situations that are detrimental or limiting us in any way will be severed during this period and we will be free to walk away with compassion, forgiveness, and total peace of mind.

In particular, we will feel the urge to remove ourselves from the company of anyone who provokes arguments, shows aggression, is controlling, manipulative, deceptive, judgmental, overly critical, or generally abusive. Basically, we will find that anything unhealthy absolutely has to be removed from our life or be totally revolutionized, whether it is relationship dynamics, careers, eating habits, or overall lifestyle choices.

Not only will we be ending a ten-year cycle that has been emotionally and mentally challenging, we are also about to embark on an important, transformational new phase, moving toward a brand-new decade—so it is vital we clear out old energy once and for all and be energetically ready for this shift.

During this 12:12 energy portal, we will be feeling compelled to evaluate and ponder over prominent things we have been through over the last ten years. In recent weeks we may also have noticed we have been repeating the same patterns over and over and attracting the same old lessons we thought we'd learned long ago.

We will be receiving numerous insights and significant aha moments alongside melancholic feelings and emotions that cause us to return and relive certain periods from the last decade that caused us confusion, turmoil, and pain.

The main reason for this is that healing, conclusions, and closure always arrive at the end of a major energy cycle, when our repressed emotions and feelings have been given a safe space to resurface and receive validation and permission to move onward.

It is essential that before we begin a fresh cycle we end old outdated ones.

The next couple of weeks will serve as an important and necessary transformational phase, and it is vital we are prepared for this shift.

Here are a few ways to release the residual karmic energies of the last decade and create an opening for the new experiences and opportunities coming our way in 2020.

Clearing out our living space is a powerful way to kick-start a flow of energy that helps keep our mind calm and clear and also invites fresh positive energy to enter. As well as clearing old energy from our personal space, we can also do the same with our electronic devices. We often keep hold of old messages or contacts or particular quotes that held intense emotional meaning at a certain time in our lives.

As we move toward a new year, this is the opportune time to remove anything that is triggering painful memories that we would rather not be regularly reminded of. If our phone is filled with text messages, photographs, or hurt and torment from the past, we can take a few moments to delete whatever causes discomfort or turmoil and clear the energy so we release whatever was not meant to be and start optimistically looking ahead.

The easiest and most healing way to let go of the past is to forgive. This means forgiving ourselves along with anyone else who may have caused us turmoil. Whenever we hold onto resentment, we remain energetically connected to the person with whom the encounter involved. By letting go of any negative emotions, we also untie the knot that was subconsciously holding us hostage. When we forgive, we effectively release and let go.

Focus time and dedication on finishing any projects that have been started or that are halfway completed. Anything that we have been procrastinating will need some kind of structure so we can release the energy caught up in it, even if all we do is make a plan with a realistic deadline.

Hand over to the Universe all fears, grudges, doubts, resentments, attachments to outcomes, perceived wrong turns and mistakes. Allow karmic energy to remind, reprimand, or reward, as the Universe sees fit.

Despite the challenges and trials this year has brought us, we can work through our karmic energy and close the year knowing that we are more awakened, consciously aware, alert, open, accountable, and authentic than ever before. Nothing is coincidence, everything that happens, every person we have a connection with, and every feeling occurs for a divine and sacred reason.

This is a time for major elimination and creation, so set intentions and believe that in 2020 you deserve to receive everything you desire and dream of. Have faith in this transition, as incredible possibilities, greatness, and blessings are most definitely on the way. 🙏 💝

I am well aware that as you read this book we may well be into 2021 as my completion of this work and the typical eighteen-month turnaround time for publishing cannot be avoided. Please take a moment and look back on your 2020, the creation of a new decade of light, and ask yourself if any of this applied. I believe you will be quite surprised, if not relieved as well that it was all in energetic and Divine order. And so it always is.

Chapter 10
Taking Back Your Power

You may be asking yourself, "What does that mean, Cat? Taking back your power?" This statement has so very many implications energetically, emotionally, mentally, spiritually, and even with your physical health and state of well-being.

When you continue to complain, discuss, and focus on a particular person and situation, you are dispersing your life force energy and leaving it with that person thus causing you to be fragmented. This person may also be leaving their energy with you as they rehash the situation and leave their energetic feelings in your energy field. This can intrude on your energetic chakra system and auric field creating dis-ease, pain, illness, and fatigue, just to name a few results, with the direct affect on your physical body.

Your emotional body (your feelings of righteousness, being violated, disrespected) will lead to anger, resentment, frustration, and upset. Your mental body will replay the entire incident in your head with you as the victim continuing to stay in the energy of the incident and NOT standing in your power.

Here's an example. We have another incidence

of adult children (laughs) emotionally abusing their parents. Each parent has children from separate relationships and they are both being attacked by false accusations and gossip spread throughout the family. They end up arguing with each other, fighting over how to handle their adult children, causing a breakdown in their marriage and relationship.

Both adult children are using the grandchildren to attempt manipulation by withholding visits. Attempts were continuously made to defend themselves thus giving away their power. As mentioned previously, when you're enrolled in responding, you're defending yourself, which says you believe what's being said. Otherwise, why would you defend yourself? When stepping back and observing their families, they can watch the game instead of feel the need to play in it. It's very obvious that these are adults who were raised with no boundaries whatsoever. This is where personal responsibility comes in and forgiveness enters the picture, releasing the hurt, anger, and disappointment. Forgiveness of self for being disempowered and victimized.

Learning to detach from the situation, being unenrolled in the conversation and enpowered, allows freedom from chaos and brings peace. This is detachment with no expectation of an outcome. I get it, you may not see your grandchildren for an extended period of time. But, giving in to manipulation will never change a situation. Take back your power and set boundaries for what is and is not acceptable to you.

When they stopped arguing with each other

and focused on the health of their relationship and marriage, things improved vastly. When not responding to the grown adults' accusations, gossip, or threats, they stopped! Of course, as what they were doing was no longer effective.

Chapter 11
Sexuality as Control

I experienced such great joy and gratitude when this participant joined our group in "Forgiveness Workshop." I had not seen her in nearly four years since she had left my Chios Energy Healing Level-Two class with health issues. Thank you, Spirit.

Imagine you're in your early thirties and you are void of all memories before the age of twenty. When your mother supports you in starting Life/Spiritual Advisement (with yours truly), she breaks down and begins to share childhood trauma with you that you had absolutely no recall of. Dissociative behavior created as a child, developed personality and survival mechanisms for protection.

Emotional abuse began in pre-school at the age of three when she was told that she "hugs too much." Boys were punching her in the first grade, and in third grade a very emotionally abusive teacher was demeaning her at every opportunity. What perceptions of self are being formed as a foundation for future living? Can you imagine?!

Don't be affectionate, loving, or vulnerable. It's not safe to express yourself or to love. I'm not good enough. I'm bad and wrong. I'm unlovable. To reinforce these thoughtforms, at a very young age she fell upon pornography of her father's and also became aware that her father was stepping out on her mother. By the fifth grade, she was laying naked with boys and when caught, was ripped away and made to feel bad, wrong, and dirty.

Could this have possibly been a way of "acting out and experiencing" what her father liked, what got his attention? He was often absent as he worked two jobs. Was this a way to connect to him or was this merely a way for a child to cry out for the time and attention of her father?

Perception of being a woman was formed at a very young age. Women are for play, not to be respected. They have no value. I don't want to be a woman, no power. Don't touch me before I choose to touch you first. Her mother never addressed her father's affair and continued to avoid asking for any communication or requesting any relationship support.

Within her childhood, there was no display of intimacy or affection between her parents. They would put her in the middle and talk behind each other's backs looking to her for validation. By the age of ten, she developed endometriosis.

"Looking at the emotional trauma/metaphysical aspects associated with this dis-ease [from *Metaphysical Anatomy* by Evette Rose] it is suppressed creativity and passion in life. You might have a fear of having children, as your own childhood experiences were traumatic. You have a fear your childhood history will repeat itself. You may also be attached to your independence as this is where you feel most powerful.

"You might feel that being dependent on others will inevitably invite circumstances that will make you feel controlled and trapped. Your life has been consumed by responsibilities, a lack of guidance and having to fend for yourself. You seem to feel quite resentful of being female, always pulling the short end of the rope in society. You have seen women being treated unfairly, abused or disrespected in society causing you to try and avoid the same treatment.

"You are unable to access your feminine power. You feel that your foundation is brittle, there is no solid ground to fall back on whenever you are faced with challenges. This may cause you to feel very insecure, scared or unsure of your ability to cope with life. You often revert to an aggressive state to keep yourself safe and to establish clear boundaries.

"You might feel under attack (either verbally or physically) by influential females in your life. Your experience with love may be intensely traumatic, destructive and left a deep emotional scar. You want to be creative yet feel controlled, attacked or judged. You don't feel safe to truly express yourself or be loved by the people you should feel safe with. Communicating your emotions, concerns or fears was never an option. You may have been ridiculed, rejected, or taken advantage of whenever you opened yourself up and reached out for comfort and support. You had to toughen up very early in life. If you didn't then your circumstances would have mentally and emotionally consumed you."

That certainly sums up quite a few things.

As she grew older, she was exposed to gang members whistling and being inappropriate with her verbally. It was "attention" albeit negative that she may have interpreted as "they like me." Her girlfriend then went through gang initiation of sex with thirteen members. A conclusion was then made that sex makes women powerful, not healthy relationships, intimacy, or boundary setting.

A persona was created, from the time of childhood, to protect herself. Don't display affection, it's not safe. She became very masculine in the sense of use for sex but dump before ninety days. It gave her all the power and control over her contact with men. She was filled with rage and if you did not respond to her in the way she wanted, she would get violent or have sex with someone else and discard the other person. This also guaranteed that no one would get close to her as she was not going to allow herself to be vulnerable in any way.

Yet what truly lies at the core of all of this is what every human wants, which is to be loved. Her promiscuity from an early age was an outcry of self-abuse and self-loathing, which started the roller-coaster of physical dis-ease stemming from insecurity, disappointment, and frustration. She had a false sense of being powerful and desirable. She loathed being a woman and created a male persona of emotional unavailability. Much work was needed in self-love and self-respect.

She was then diagnosed with a rare dis-ease called vasculitis, which is an inflammatory disease of blood vessels that can affect any number of organs. The immune system attacks the blood vessels. This can be triggered by infection, medication, or another disorder such as chronic Hepatitis B or C.

As stated in *Metaphysical Anatomy* by Yvette Rose, "you seem to feel that your truth has been manipulated by influential people's own values or beliefs. You have experienced a 'hardening of the attitude' as an unconscious effort to emotionally protect yourself from others. You are simmering with anger as a result of love that has been denied.

"You felt deprived of many privileges during childhood. You feel there is a lack of love, support, encouragement and protection in your life. You are resentful as you couldn't have what you wanted in relationships. You feel punished, as if you were treated unfairly.

"You are holding on to old grudges from the past. You firmly believe that what comes around, goes around. You want to see others get what they have coming, especially those who caused you pain, trauma or upset. You are stubborn when you are faced with circumstances that push you to take responsibility for the future and how you are currently feeling. You have given your power away to others and are deeply resentful. You seem to be blaming others for this situation.

"You feel challenged by life and may feel that you do not have what it takes to achieve your goals. You don't feel important in the eyes of the people you love. You struggle and fight just to be seen and acknowledged.

"You may have made an association that love disempowers you. You are unconsciously fighting against everyone that comes too close to your heart. How does keeping others at arms- length keep you safe? Who made you feel this way in the past?

"You have suppressed feeling compassion toward yourself. You have abandoned the idea that life can be easy as your experience has been very different. Who or what made you feel this way?

"Love and affection may have been shown to you in an angry, aggressive, or resentful way. What would happen if you had to let go of resentments and grudges towards others? How does it serve you to feel these strong emotions?

"Explore the need for vengeance or for blaming others for how you feel. Feeling overwhelmed with many responsibilities at an early age. Why? How did this make you feel? What would happen if you started to focus more on your own life instead of others? You may feel that many responsibilities, stress, tension, deprivation=love and acceptance.

"Explore the difference between your stress or anger and your parent's or ancestor's emotions. You might feel that love will only weaken you. If relevant, and receiving love.

"How does being emotionally hard serve you? What does it protect you from? How has this attitude served you in the past? What/who does it protect you from? In which area of your life do you feel stagnant and angry? Why? What happened and how did that make you feel?"

These are some very heavy emotions, experiences, and situations that had to be addressed for true healing to occur on all levels ... physical, emotional, mental, and spiritual. This was a journey of establishing boundaries, self-love, self-respect, forgiveness of self and others, accountability, and reconnection to her powerful Divine Feminine energy. This all started in the Forgiveness Workshop.

This next chapter is written by our participant from her perspective as to the impact of doing her work, which started with the Forgiveness Workshop and the Forgiveness Formula.

Chapter 12
Personal Transformation

I start this chapter with a personal acknowledgment of my participant's willingness to share, be authentic, and be vulnerable so others may benefit from her life experiences. This takes selflessness and tremendous growth and maturity. This section is written by her personally.

"In 2014, I took a Chios Energy Healing Class in Wheaton, IL taught by Cat Baldwin and received my Level One Attunement (raising of frequency to be open to receive higher states of energy and pure consciousness). At the time, I was on short-term disability for vasculitis and during my time off, was exploring alternative therapies to the western standard.

"Fast forward to 2017 where I found myself on full disability, getting back on track health-wise, and I once again was looking to invest some time and energy on spiritual growth. Around Thanksgiving, I checked-out meetup.com and found that Cat had a 'Forgiveness Workshop From Higher Self/Spirit' going on the following week. I assumed this class was going to meet once or twice on this topic, but I was way off. They had been in session weekly since September and this was an ongoing weekly Workshop.

"This was the beginning of the journey that I am currently pursuing, resulting in positive life shifting changes. Just like in Chios Class, I felt Spirit brought the group of students together because after the first class, I felt confidence with the ladies. That was not typical for me.

"Even though there was an age difference with my other classmates, I never felt judged or treated differently. It helped cultivate a safe environment where I could shed my chameleon façade. I had spent my entire life being whom everyone else around me wanted, or who I thought they wanted.

"After a few months of being confronted with my cause in the matter, my emotional trauma and how I had ragefully and self-destructively responded to it, I realized I could further benefit with one-on-one Spiritual Counsel/Advisement with Cat. That was the shift that Spirit was waiting for me to take which then opened the floodgates to finally deal with things in my past.

"Part of my challenge in Forgiveness Workshop was my memory. Before 18 years old, I had a few images that would flash in my head but nothing similar to my peers when reminiscing about their childhood. Then from 18 to 23 is a fuzzy drug and alcohol whirlwind so not much to go on in that department as well.

"Since my mother had covered years of counseling prior to this, going to her to ask for financial support on this occasion wasn't unusual.

What was different was the diarrhea of the mouth that she exhibited the day she agreed to cover it. I learned details of my childhood that helped to explain part of the traumatic shutdown mode my mind went in.

"The fantastic part, a true blessing (yes that's what I said), was that I finally had things to go on, overcome and deal with it, instead of guessing what happened to me. Needless to say, we had a good amount to sift through, but the headway of the personal sessions and Workshop was a wonderful collaboration that only Spirit could have organized!

"When I began Forgiveness Workshop, I had a 90-day dating rule with men. After 90, we're done. According to my medical charts, I had 12 different dis-ease diagnosis. I could easily sleep with any male or female to get what I wanted. I was taking 34 medications daily, I had substance abuse issues, and my forgiveness list consisted of 16 people. I really felt I had a good handle on my life (this was actually control to ensure my safety), had a huge amount of 'friends' and dealt with situations like a 'good little soldier.'

"Since I made all the decisions that shaped the roads I wandered, working on forgiveness helped release all the negative associations I had with those choices. My forgiveness letter to myself after 8 months of Workshop … I apologize for being so hard on myself and not accepting help. I was more comfortable to shove everything and everyone away and carve 'I hate you' on my stomach than ask for someone to help me do anything.

"My childhood experience of dismissal of concerns and absolute lack of acknowledgement and support, created this way of being. This is how my mother treated herself. She would not communicate her hurt or concerns to my father as she was more empowered being a victim and making him wrong for past offenses. Instead of forgiving, he was and continues to be in a no-win situation. He will always be judged from his past no matter what efforts he makes so she can continue to have an excuse for pity and for not allowing herself to love him.

"Even though I grew-up in a house where the adults still do not address the core of their relationship issues, I decided that I wanted to improve my communication skills because I have been frightened my entire life of ending up like my parents. In a poem I wrote when I was 10, I wished there was peace in the world and we lived in a place where husband and wife loved each other.

"I never played wedding dress-up as a child, nor did I want children. I started babysitting at 12 and enjoyed playing with the children and handling the responsibility. But possibly, I didn't want to raise a child thinking that the model of relationships I had been raised in was the standard. I agree with Evette Rose in *Metaphysical Anatomy* because I had a fear that my childhood history would repeat itself.

"And I quote, 'You might feel that being dependent on others will inevitably invite circumstances that will make you feel controlled and trapped. Your life has been consumed by responsibilities, a lack of guidance and having to fend for yourself. You seem to feel quite resentful of being a female, always pulling the short end of the rope in society. You have seen women being treated unfairly, abused or disrespected in society causing you to try to avoid the same treatment.'

"My mother raised me 'overly strong' her words not mine. Spiteful towards men would be mine for the choosing. Unfortunately, she never embraced her own femininity. When I was in grade school, I used to have happy dreams where my parents would get divorced so there could be peace in the home. I don't believe that until recently, did they both realize that they used me from a very young age, as the mediator between them and within the family unit.

"I cannot begin to imagine all that they have gone through in their lifetimes and the real truth behind stories that I am aware of. I have completed my Forgiveness Formula questions around my relationship with my parents. I know they did the best they could with the tools they had. Wounded inner children raise wounded inner children.

"That being said, I believe I came out of the womb hating men. I was an OG tomboy, which the more I begin to recall feels like an early indication of how resentful I was being female. When I would ask my mom questions, the response I would get quite frequently was that no one showed her something or explained something to her. By her not taking ownership of being a responsible adult, learning to fill in the gaps, I feel the switch of mother/daughter role began to flip. I am certain as a child that I resented taking the role of the house matron.

"One of the images I can remember as clear as day is going outside to tell her something must be seriously wrong. I was so frightened. On my 9th birthday, my menstrual cycle started. All I knew was that I was bleeding. I was confused and did not know what was happening. I had to ask older girls on the block who had more experience. With the lack of guidance and me feeling that I had to fend for myself, inadvertently tossed me to the wolves. Is it a huge wonder that I was promiscuous and experimenting with drugs before 16?

"The way I interpreted how to deal with men became more distorted after I was brutally raped in 2005. Something in my head flipped and I began to trick like every day was Halloween. If I wasn't already marching to the beat of sex and power, now I was leading the parade. Everyone was a new victim. I wanted to be put in a psyche ward to help me figure my head out, but due to public opinion I was told to suck it up and take a semester off. This semester off turned into a season of epic self-destruction mode. Even though this mode would move from a category 10 to a lower number over a decade, it wasn't until Forgiveness Workshop that the rage was acknowledged, loved and embraced and then released that I truly became the creator of my life.

"As I began to release negative emotions I had associated with certain people, I started to see the difference of people who wanted to work on their situation and those who don't want to do the necessary work. I have had close friends and family tell me they admire me working on myself because they wouldn't want to invest the time to do so.

"This sounds so ridiculous to me but as I have learned as a great comeback to others, 'I get how that is for you.' We are all on our own spiritual journey and in different places. I'm only responsible for me.

"As it stands today, I have been abstinent for a year, I am down to 5 different diagnosis and six medications and 18 months since I've touched anything stronger than medical marijuana. I have a small authentic group of friends, and I take a good breath before responding rather than reacting to situations. My forgiveness list consists of a running total of 318 people. I have learned to let go and not attempt to control everything. Now I truly know what it authentically feels like to have a good handle on myself and my life, living with discernment, self-love, boundaries and integrity.

"To follow are 3 letters that I wrote while engaging in the Forgiveness Workshop.

"Letter for an X-boyfriend 2008

"He showed me that monogamy was possible. That I actually could be loved for me. I was able to depend on someone and they would/could help me. He changed the script and gave me the experience of being loved. He did his job well and I thank him for that. When I make a decision, I have to own all repercussions. He led me to search for Higher Power, my Truth and the potential of the real me.

"My attacker from 2005

"He helped me by physically assaulting me so that I could end up helping so many other men and women who had endured the same. During a session in March 2020 with Cat, it also came to light that this is what it felt to be violated. I had been physically and emotionally violating people in the past with no concern for the consequences of what it may have caused others ... whether men or women. It occurred very differently when that was done for me. For this I am truly thankful.

"Mom

"She is the best cheerleader I needed for this position in this lifetime. She is the most caring and attentive nurse I could ask for. Whatever I asked for that she was able to provide, she followed through without fail. I learned the importance of trust and communication. I learned empathy towards others. For this I am truly thankful."

Chapter 13
Emotions vs. Feelings

In *The Jeshua Channelings: Christ Consciousness in a New Era* by Pamela Kribbe, Jeshua teaches us that "Emotions are energies that are essentially expressions of misunderstanding. Feelings are a form of higher understanding and are generated from heart consciousness. (our Heart Lock-In experience).

"Emotions always have something very intense and dramatic to them. Emotions take hold of you completely and pull you away from your spiritual center, your inner clarity. Feelings, on the other hand, bring you deeper into yourself, into your center. Feelings are closely associated with intuition, expressing a higher understanding that transcends both the emotions and the mind. They originate in a non-physical realm outside of the body.

"Feelings originate from the dimension of your Higher or Greater Self. You need to be quiet inside to catch those whispers in your heart. Emotions can disturb this inner silence and peace. Therefore, it is vital to become emotionally calm and to heal and release repressed emotions. Only from your feeling which connects you to your soul can you make balanced decisions.

"By being quiet and peaceful, you can feel with all of your being what is right for you at a certain moment. Making decisions based on emotions is making decisions from a non-centered position. You need to release the emotion first and get in touch with your inner core where there is clarity.

"Your emotions are directly related to your inner child (unresolved trauma). Emotions can best be viewed as an energy that comes to you for healing. Therefore, it is important to not be swept completely away by the emotion, but to remain able to look at it from a neutral stance. It is important to stay conscious.

"One might put it like this; you should not repress an emotion but should not drown in it either. For when you drown in it, when you identify with it completely, the child in you becomes a tyrant that will lead you astray. Allow it in, feel all aspects of it while not losing your consciousness.

"Take for instance anger. You can invite anger to be fully present, experiencing it in your body at several places, while you are at the same time neutrally observing it. Such a type of consciousness is healing. What happens in this instance is that you embrace this emotion, which is essentially a form of misunderstanding, with understanding. This is spiritual alchemy.

"Turning towards your emotions in such a loving manner is liberating. It does require a kind of self-discipline. Releasing outside reality as the 'source of the evil' and taking full responsibility yourself means that you acknowledge that 'you chose to react in a certain way.' You stop arguing about who is right and who is wrong, who is to blame for what and you simply release the whole chain of events that happened outside of your control. 'I now experience this emotion in the full awareness that I choose to do so.' That is taking responsibility. That takes courage.

"This is the self-discipline that is asked of you. At the same time, this kind of turning inward requires the highest compassion. The emotion you are honestly prepared to face as your own creation is also looked upon with gentle understanding. 'You chose anger this time didn't you?' Compassion tells you: 'Okay. I can see why and I forgive you. Perhaps when you feel my love and support more clearly you will not feel inclined to take that response next time.'

"This is the true role of consciousness in self-healing. This is what spiritual alchemy means. Consciousness does not fight or reject anything. It encircles darkness with awareness. It encircles the energies of misunderstanding with understanding and thus transforms ordinary metal into gold. Consciousness and love are essentially the same. Being conscious means letting something be and surrounding it with your love and compassion.

"Often you think that 'consciousness alone' is not enough to overcome your emotional problems. You say: I know I have repressed emotions, I know the cause of it, I am aware but it does not go away.

"In that case, there is a subtle resistance within you to that emotion. You keep the emotion at a distance, for fear of being overwhelmed by it. But you are never overwhelmed by an emotion when you consciously chose to allow it.

"As long as you keep the emotion at a distance, you are at war with it. You are fighting the emotion and it will turn against you in several ways. You cannot keep it outside in the end. It will manifest itself in the body as an ache, a tension or as a feeling of depression. Feeling down or weary is frequently a sign that you are repressing certain emotions.

"The thing is that you need to allow the emotions to fully enter your consciousness. If you do not know exactly what emotions are there, you can very well start by feeling the tensions in your body. This is a gateway to the emotions. In your body it is all stored. For instance, if you feel pain or tension in the area of your stomach, you can go there with your awareness and ask what is the matter. Let the cells of your body speak to you. Or imagine, that right there, a child is present. Ask the child to show you what is emotion is predominant in him or her.

"There are several ways to connect with your emotions. It is vital to realize that the energy got stuck in the emotion <u>wants</u> to move. This energy wants to be released and therefore it knocks on your door as a physical complaint or as a feeling of stress or depression. For you it is merely a matter of you opening-up and being prepared to feel the emotion.

"Emotions are part of your earthly reality, but they should not get a hold over you. Emotions are like clouds for the sun. Therefore, it is so important to be aware of your emotions and to deal with them consciously. From a clear and balanced emotional body, it is much easier to contact your soul or inner core through your intuition.

"It is very important to take responsibility for your own emotions and not to make absolute truths of them. When you give them the status of truths, instead of looking upon them as 'explosions of misunderstanding' you will base your actions on them and that will lead to uncentered decisions.

"You can very well observe inside of you whether there are emotions that you cherish in such a way that you regard them as truth instead of what they really are: explosions of misunderstanding. These are emotions you have identified with. The paradox is, that often enough, these are emotions that cause you much suffering. For instance: powerlessness ('I cannot help it'), control ('I'll handle it'), anger ('It's their fault'), or grief ('Life is miserable'). These are all emotions that are painful but yet, on another level, they give you something special to hold on to.

"Take powerlessness or the 'victim feeling.' There can be advantages to this emotional pattern. It may give you a sense of safety. It releases you from certain obligations or responsibilities. 'I can't help it, can I?' It is a dark corner you are sitting in, but it seems a safe one. The danger of identifying or 'merging' with such an emotional pattern for a long time is that you lose touch with your own true freedom, your innermost divine core.

"Things may have entered your life path that have justifiably provoked emotions of anger and resentment within you. This may have happened in your youth, later on or even in past lives. It is very important that you get in touch with these emotions consciously and that you become aware of the anger, sadness or any other intensely charged energy within you. But at a certain point you need to take responsibility for your emotions, for they constitute your reactions to an outside event.

"Being centered, being in a state of clarity and spiritual balance, means that you take full responsibility for all the emotions that are in you. You can then recognize the emotion of, for instance, anger within you and say at the same time: this was my reaction to certain events. I surround this reaction with understanding, but at the same time I intend to release it.

"Life is ultimately not about being right; it is about being free and whole. It is very liberating to release old emotional responses that have grown into a lifestyle.

"One might say it is all about the subtle middle road between suppressing emotions and drowning in them. On both sides, you have been raised with opinions and ideals that are not in accordance with the nature of spiritual alchemy. The essence of spiritual growth is that you do not suppress anything, but at the same time you take full responsibility for it. I feel this, I choose this reaction, so I can heal it. Claiming your mastership—that is what my message is about truly.

"Claim your mastership, become the master of the emotional bits and pieces that torment you, often behind your back. Get in touch with them, take responsibility. Don't let yourself be driven by unconscious emotional hurts that sidetrack you and block your road to inner freedom. It is your consciousness that heals. No one else can restore the power over your own emotions for you. There are no external instruments or means to take away those emotions. It is in becoming aware of them with strength, determination and compassion that they are released into the Light.

"Becoming whole and free on the emotional level is one of the most important aspects of growing spiritually. I want to finish by saying: do not make it more difficult than it is. The spiritual path is a simple path. It is about love for yourself and inner clarity. It does not require any specific knowledge or any specific rituals, rules or methods. All things you need for your spiritual growth are within you."

Can you now clearly see that YOU determine if you are going to be a prisoner of your emotions and experiences. It is up to you to pursue your mastership. It is up to you to heal you. Will you distract yourself with outside activities and busyness to not feel what is hidden from you? Will you love yourself and pursue your greatness with self-forgiveness and forgiveness of others? It is all here for your benefit, for your growth, for your transformation. Will you love and embrace all of it?

Chapter 14
Adversity = Thank You

Further opportunity to put this into practice was given to me AGAIN as it has been many times before. Please be clear. I do not just facilitate what Spirit is presenting. I MUST live it, experience it, and heal it for the benefit of myself and the spiritual community.

A brutal, overcast Midwest winter came with no end in sight. "We had a water pipe break on the second floor. It looks like a waterfall. You need to come in and check your unit right away. It's very bad." Can you imagine receiving this phone call? I did on Friday, February 1, 2019, when my landlord called me with this information. This is the building where I had my practice.

Breathing deeply, as I had a thirty-minute drive before I arrived, I calmed myself. My unit was in the lower level. I was certain it was divinely protected as my facility belonged to Archangel Metatron and several of my Ascended Masters. When I arrived and entered my facility, all was intact and dry with the exception of one-half inch of water on the floor, which all my area rugs had soaked up. NOTHING was damaged.

The remainder of the building was another

story completely and as I would soon find out, the repairs before resumed occupancy could be up to six months. The Universe had given me a major curve ball and now it was up to me as to how I would respond, from ego or my heart/soul, with fear, anger, and upset or with forgiveness as this was a major gift to me.

Oh, yes, seeing that when you're in the middle of all this? That's a totally different story. That's just being human. For the majority of my life, I had shoved down emotions and barreled through as that was what I was taught to do. Be strong. Sound familiar?

The fear (false expectations appearing real) moved in immediately. Where am I going to practice? How am I going to serve my community? After a phone call with a trusted colleague, it was pointed out to me that I certainly had room at my home and could travel with my table to perform in-home healing treatments. The emotion of fear, deeply rooted in emotional/physical abandonment in my childhood, had reared its ugly head to be addressed. One of several core wounds, which I had thought I had healed, were soon to be brought to the surface in a big, attention-getting way!

Contacting everyone, they all agreed to attend treatments and classes at the house. So blessed, I took a deep breath. I set out to find a new location, as Spirit was clearly telling me it was time to move on. I had almost left this location in October, but circumstances were not lining up although I did feel I had found the area where I would like to relocate.

I had been waiting for my landlord to create a new one-year-only lease and had requested it on several occasions to no avail. His behavior had been deceptive and somewhat curious over the past several months. Spirit very loudly said, "No lease. Don't ask again." Obviously, there was a reason for that!

I returned to the area I had been considering, found the space I wanted, and started the ball rolling. Everything in the old location was moved to one room and covered in plastic where I was certain it would be protected until I was ready to move out. Keep in mind, I had no lease.

One week later, sitting on my couch, the room started to spin. I became nauseous and vomited my morning smoothie. Within twenty-four hours, I was at the ER diagnosed with H1N1 swine flu. I had not been sick in twenty years, not even a cold. Over the next ten days, I was in the ER twice with dizziness and vomiting, fever of 103. This healing process was five weeks long. I could not eat or even get off the couch let alone think about helping anyone else. Looking for lessons or the benefit in adversity can be challenging during something like this, to say the least!

When Spirit cannot get your attention, they will knock you right upside the head to varying degrees. Many lessons and messages came through during this time frame. First and foremost, forgiveness. Everything is done "for" you, not "to" you. I was also very clearly being shown that I was not alone. Two of my spiritual community took me to the ER, brought me food, and checked in on me daily. Others stepped forward to grocery shop and assist my son with his needs.

Spirit was very clear about many things, as I was awoken every morning at 6:00 with intense anxiety. I have never had anxiety in my life. I was instructed to breathe deeply and be in the present moment, a practice I had established for myself over fifteen years ago. I was to put my self-care first, before anything or anyone else, sending myself love and compassion daily, not just now but from this point forward. A three-week fever was to clear and burn out all the negative energy in my energy field. I was not clearing myself and I perform healings on people daily.

As much as I take very good care of myself physically, with supplementation nutrition smoothies and I have been a vegetarian at their request for nine years, Spirit was very clear that my emotional/spiritual well-being must be addressed daily. Physical is a must, focus on emotional, and the spirit body was now being emphasized. Forgive myself as I am human and emotions are to be felt, experienced, and healed. To have a negative emotion does not mean that I am not on my spiritual path. It means that I am human.

For those of you who, like myself, are intuitive/empaths you may be aware that we have been clearing the collective consciousness for our entire lives. "No more clean-up in Aisle 7." Spirit was clear that we had completed our requested assistance and now it is all about us as individual lightworkers. We are here to heal ourselves FIRST.

My core wounds of my inner child had not been fully healed. When ignoring emotions, we are invalidating the feelings of the inner child. As these core wounds are still showing up when activated by a particular situation, this is a clear indicator that more work needs to be done. Trust me ... it never ends. If you think you have done it all and it's all healed, that would be your ego speaking (laugh).

When we are activated with fear, abandonment, mistrust (negative emotions), these are deep-core inner-child wounds. Inner-child work was not given as an option. Although I have been working on myself for forty-six years, there was more work to be done. We all have deeply rooted emotions and thoughtforms that were put there by well-meaning friends, parents, and teachers. They remain taking up space in the center of your head until addressed (more on that later).

The request was also made from Spirit to create an Inner Child Workshop. We are all wounded children, it's merely to what degree. I continue daily all requests made by Spirit as I know they are for my highest and greatest good.

On April 1, only two months after this all began, the keys to our new facility were handed to me. A buildout which was scheduled for three more weeks out, was done in three days when another project had fallen through. I had contacted a painter on Friday with no expectation of him meeting me with two days' notice. Not only did he meet me the day I took possession, but he finished the painting in less than two days.

Within a week, everything was moved and set up and I was back in my practice. I was out of the basement, away from noise and aggravation and limited parking to a beautiful, peaceful facility with two windows, abundant parking, and surrounded by beautiful woods that we can utilize anytime for class, meditation, or just enjoyment. Adversity = Thank You! I chose to forgive myself for initial lack of trust that my highest good was being served. I am grateful to my landlord for not renewing my lease and for the water pipe bursting to push me forward to a place much more suited to the communities increasing vibrational frequency and growth.

This is where the creation of this book began and for THIS I am truly thankful.

Chapter 15
The New Earth

As I complete this my second book, our planet is in the midst of the greatest transformation in our history. So many of us have been waiting lifetimes for this grand occurrence, healing and holding energy for the Earth and humanity. The Ascended Masters, Archangels, and Elohim have been waiting aeons. We are all on lockdown due to the coronavirus. I am aware that we are well past this as publishing upon acceptance can take up to eighteen months from print to purchase.

Spirit has requested we have a conversation concerning exactly what is happening in "The Shift." I am certainly hoping to look back at this time and visibly see the great changes that have occurred in this challenging time. The virus, as everything, is a blessing and in Divine Order, uniting us in one global heart with the suffering of all people, everywhere. This is a global pandemic, as it was labeled by the media. Although, due to their overdramatic sensationalism, panic, fear, and in the beginning, the worst of humanity was displayed.

The self-centered hoarding of toilet paper, antibacterial wipes, diapers, and food displayed the level of work that we as humanity must diligently get started on. Of course, this is all ego-based fear, certainly not Spirit-based love. We don't want to be inconvenienced or pushed out of our distraction comfort zone. We now even fear getting sick.

When in faith, we know we are divinely provided for and would not put our individual needs before the needs of the masses/collective. There is plenty for everyone in a country with tremendous resources, strengths, and funding. At the request of Spirit, during the first ten days of this, I continued in deep meditation to clear the mass consciousness/collective of fear and anxiety. The energies were so heavy that I was completely exhausted. Daily, love, healing, and light continue to be sent to all including Mother Earth. I requested the same of my community.

As time has progressed, it is softer and lighter as we embrace what's so and what is being requested of us. Many have lost their jobs, many are working from home, and all are wondering how we will ever recover from this economically as families, a nation, and the world. Will we recover as a society and embrace all the blessings and abundance or will we avoid each other in fear of getting sick? Will we continue the "us" vs. "them" of ignorance or embrace each other with joy as we thrive on human contact and hugs?

Those on lockdown are constantly seeking things to "do" in an effort to distract themselves from the situation and the emotions associated with it. And yet, this may work for a short period of time, as one of the purposes of "The Shift" is to awaken the mass consciousness to truth, love, and a new way of "being," not "doing." The planet is ascending as are we as humanity from third-dimensional frequency to four- and five-dimensional frequency. There is NOTHING that can stop this. We have been given this time to go within, center ourselves, reconnect to Source, heal ourselves, and create something newly known as the Golden Age/New Earth.

Each and every one of us agreed to participate in this "great experiment," an experiment of ego-based programming, image-generated self-value, consumerism, and self-importance. Ultimately, Source wanted to experience the duality of the Earth plan and we all agreed to provide this as we wanted the experience as well. Without duality such as hate, we would not know love, right and wrong, us and them. We ultimately would not be moved to step back into our divine selves as the spark of Divinity that each of us is. The experience of the 3D duality has provided the space for lessons, healing, and the return to our Spirit selves. Whether conscious of it or not, everyone is awakening at this time.

Mother Earth selflessly hosted our experiment in consciousness, compromising her very well-being. She can no longer sustain herself with our pollution, disregard for sentient beings (all animal life), disconnection from our very selves with ignorance to the amount of garbage we produce with our mass consumerism attempting to fill the voids within us with "things" when all we need lies within us. We take for granted all she provides; our food, water, shelter, and even the beauty of her peace when spent in her presence. This is a global call to love. If we refuse, she herself will begin rebelling with hurricanes, volcano eruptions, tidal waves, tsunamis, and more devastation than we can even consider.

Ugly and heinous things will be revealed. Systems of control and manipulation that have been here for thousands of years have kept us distracted and busy with acquiring material things. This leaves no time to pursue your spiritual life and Higher Self. It keeps us in the constant loop of repetitive survival behaviors and dependency. Trust me, this was perpetrated on humanity for this particular purpose. Some will understand and some will deny. Some will refuse to think that they have been manipulated and have no conscious knowledge of it whatsoever.

There is discomfort when something is "unfamiliar." But this is what I know. We are all powerful beings of light and love, more powerful than we can ever conceive. Our human "Spirit" is strong, resilient, and we are all a spark of Source, "All That Is," which is pure love. As time has progressed, I see the beauty of others taking care of the elders' needs, sewing face masks, companies creating ventilators that normally do not. When we are challenged, the very best of us does come out.

A clean, beautiful planet, everyone with shelter/food, mental health issues embraced with love, compassion, and healing (no longer ignored), and each of us thriving, joyful, and loved. As I close this book and chapter, I have full faith in all of us. I am excited by what is possible and the co-creation with Spirit of the New Earth. Are you?

My heart centered desire for you is that you benefit from this work as much as I and my participants have. I wish you healing, joy, and peace on your road of forgiveness, growth, and expansion to your Spirit Self.

Until we meet again, I love each and every one of you.

CAT

Forgiveness Workshop From Higher Self/Spirit Workbook

Let the healing begin!!

This Workshop will support you in moving out of the ego's control and into your Higher Self/ Spirit. One of the most powerful ways to do this is through forgiveness. When the ego chimes in with the chatter, and trust me it will throughout this process, the response is simple. Say out loud or to yourself, "Yes, I get that and thank you for sharing. That's not my truth any longer. Thank you for all you have provided. My soul and my heart space are expanding. I scoop you up and return you to Source with love. No fear, only love."

Let us begin with a heart-based meditation from the Heart Math Institute, utilized before Workshop and throughout your day for three to five minutes, whenever possible.

Step 1. Focus your attention in the area of the heart. Imagine your breath is flowing in and out of your heart or chest area, breathing a little slower and deeper than usual.

Step 2. Activate and sustain a regenerative

feeling such as appreciation, care, or compassion.

Step 3. Radiate that renewing feeling to yourself and others.

One of the biggest benefits of learning to follow your heart's promptings will be the ability to bring your mental and emotional faculties into greater alignment with your true self. Did you send appreciation, care, and compassion to yourself? If not, why not? You DESERVE it.

"I am at peace. I am safe. I love and appreciate myself. All is well."

List everyone who you feel needs forgiveness and please write the emotion which this person evokes in you. Do not spare anyone (laughs). Pick the top five people that had the greatest impact on you and along with the emotions, please answer "The Forgiveness Formula" questions as thoroughly as possible. You may then move on with your list of people and the emotions associated with each. If you feel the need to really dig into each person and write an extensive experience using "The Forgiveness Formula" questions then please do so.

I have a list that encompassed 60 people, and I have seen lists that encompass over 150. The point of this is not to point fingers or blame, it is to heal from a higher perspective than your ego, from your Higher Self and truly release victimization and embrace growth and expansion.

The Forgiveness Formula questions as addressed through Higher/Self and Spirit.

1. Instead of asking what has someone done TO you, consider what they have done FOR you.
2. Did they do their jobs well?
3. What did they teach you and what was/is the lesson?
4. Overcome your human response of judgment, blame, and self-righteousness and embrace with unconditional love and gratitude all that has been provided for you.

Please begin with a letter to yourself.

_____
_____
_____
_____
_____
_____
_____
_____
_____
_____
_____
_____
_____
_____
_____
_____

_____

_____

_____

_____

_____

_____

_____

_____

_____

_____

_____

_____

_____

_____

_____

"I am perfect, whole, and complete at every moment."

Pick the top   five people who   need your forgiveness and the emotion associated with that person, applying "The Forgiveness Formula" questions.

_____

_____

_____

_____

_____

_____
_____
_____
_____
_____
_____
_____
_____
_____
_____
_____
_____
_____
_____
_____
_____
_____
_____
_____
_____
_____
_____
_____
_____
_____
_____
_____
_____
_____
_____
_____

"I bring joy to my heart and express love to all."

_____
_____
_____
_____
_____
_____
_____
_____
_____
_____
_____
_____
_____
_____
_____
_____
_____
_____
_____

"It is safe for me to express and release my emotions. I love myself."

The key is to really sit with this emotion, allow it to come to the surface, breathe deeply, and see it release. Visualize the emotion in words, fill with white light, and transmute them to the words light and love. And again, when these emotions get re-activated/triggered by other occurrences in your life, these relationships may have been the point of origin. The emotion/thoughtform has not been fully released from the programming or experience. Get in touch with the emotion and do it again. Consistent Chios Energy Healing sessions to clear these layers as they are exposed is recommended whether with me personally at my facility or via distance healing.

Many of these emotions are being activated by our Wounded Inner Child. You will get in touch with these emotions as you work through your family. The Wounded Inner Child will continually poke at your stomach/digestion in an attempt to get your attention. As you do this work, please get in touch with her/him by placing your hand on your stomach, gently rubbing and visualizing yourself as a child. Bend down so you are eye-to-eye and embrace her/him. "You are amazing and I am so happy you are here. You are perfect, whole, and complete at every moment. You are safe and I will protect you. I love you unconditionally and I will never leave you. I hear you and acknowledge your feelings and we will work through this together." Please visualize big hugs and kisses between you. You have become your inner child's parent.

For many decades, some lightworkers (including myself) had the mission of clearing/ healing the mass consciousness. If you have experienced an intense emotion come over you for no apparent reason whatsoever, this is what is occurring. Please say out loud, "May all who are feeling _____ (insert the emotion you are feeling) be healed, blessed, and transformed."

"I release all that is not love."

Now continue on with your list. Go back as far as you need to.

_____

_____

_____

_____

_____

_____

_____

_____

_____

_____

_____

_____

_____

_____

_____

_____

_____

_____

_____

_____

_____

_____

_____

_____

_____
_____
_____
_____
_____
_____
_____
_____
_____
_____
_____
_____
_____
_____
_____
_____
_____
_____
_____
_____
_____

"I am the creator of my life. Empowered, a create an extraordinary life of possibility."

_____
_____
_____
_____
_____
_____
_____
_____

_____

_____

_____

_____

_____

_____

_____

_____

_____

_____

_____

_____

_____

_____

Please use these pages to journal your insights, breakthroughs, and joy!!

_____

_____

_____

_____

_____

_____

_____

_____

_____

_____

_____

_____

_____

_____

_____

_____

_____

_____

_____

I honor and acknowledge you for your commitment to stepping into your greatness. YOU are a spark of Divinity and YOU are loved.

Bibliography

Kribbe, Pamela. *The Jeshua Channelings: Christ Consciousness in a New Era.* Copyright © 2008 Pamela Kribbe.

Schwartz, Robert. *Your Soul's Gift: The Healing Power of the Life You Planned before You Were Born.* Copyright © 2012 Robert Schwartz.

Schwartz, Robert. *Your Soul's Plan: Discovering the Real Meaning of the Life You Planned before You Were Born*, published by North Atlantic Books, copyright © 2007, 2009 by Robert Schwartz. Reprinted by permission of North Atlantic Books.

Young, Wm. Paul. *The Shack.* Copyright © 2007 Wm. Paul Young, published by Windblown Media.

Recommended Reading List

Divine Gifts of Healing: My Life with Spirit by Cat Baldwin

You Can Heal your Life by Louise H. Hay

The Jeshua Channelings: Christ Consciousness in a New Era by Pamela Kribbe

Metaphysical Anatomy by Yvette Rose

Your Soul's Gift and *Your Soul's Plan* by Robert Schwartz

About the Author

In practice for 22 years, Cat Baldwin is a Vibrational Frequency Practitioner, Life/ Soul and Spiritual Advisor, Ascension School/ Spiritual Teacher, Certified Chios Master Teacher and Author/Speaker. As Owner of The Wellness Sanctuary Spiritual Teaching and Healing Center she is the facilitator of programming to heal the four-body system (mental, physical, emotional and spiritual).

As an intuitive channel, clairsentient and clairaudient she is in communication with her spiritual team of Archangel Metatron, Anubis, Mother Mary, Mary Magdalene Yeshua Ben Joseph and members of The Galactic Council to co-create services for personal sovereignty, and soul purpose living.

Books by Cat Baldwin

The Forgiveness Workshop
Published by: Ozark Mountain Publishing

Divien Gifts of Healing
Published by: Ozark Mountain Publishing

For more information about any of the above titles, soon to be released titles, or other items in our catalog, write, phone or visit our website:
Ozark Mountain Publishing, Inc.
PO Box 754, Huntsville, AR 72740
479-738-2348/800-935-0045
www.ozarkmt.com

If you liked this book, you might also like:

A Small Book of Comfort
by Lyn Willmott
Sleep Magic
by Victoria Pendragon
Being In A Body
by Victoria Pendragon
Born Healers
by Victoria Pendragon
Sleeping Phoenix
by Victoria Pendragon
Waking up In The Spiritual Age
by Dan Bird
Finding Your Way In The Spiritual Age
by Dan Bird

For more information about any of the above titles, soon to be released titles,
or other items in our catalog, write, phone or visit our website:
Ozark Mountain Publishing, LLC
PO Box 754, Huntsville, AR 72740
479-738-2348
www.ozarkmt.com

For more information about any of the titles published by Ozark Mountain Publishing, Inc., soon to be released titles, or other items in our catalog, write, phone or visit our website:

Ozark Mountain Publishing, Inc.

PO Box 754

Huntsville, AR 72740

479-738-2348/800-935-0045

www.ozarkmt.com

Other Books by Ozark Mountain Publishing, Inc.

Dolores Cannon
A Soul Remembers Hiroshima
Between Death and Life
Conversations with Nostradamus,
   Volume I, II, III
The Convoluted Universe -Book One,
   Two, Three, Four, Five
The Custodians
Five Lives Remembered
Jesus and the Essenes
Keepers of the Garden
Legacy from the Stars
The Legend of Starcrash
The Search for Hidden Sacred
   Knowledge
They Walked with Jesus
The Three Waves of Volunteers and the
   New Earth
Aron Abrahamsen
Holiday in Heaven
Out of the Archives – Earth Changes
James Ream Adams
Little Steps
Justine Alessi & M. E. McMillan
Rebirth of the Oracle
Kathryn/Patrick Andries
Naked in Public
Kathryn Andries
The Big Desire
Dream Doctor
Soul Choices: Six Paths to Find Your
   Life Purpose
Soul Choices: Six Paths to Fulfilling
   Relationships
Patrick Andries
Owners Manual for the Mind
Cat Baldwin
Divine Gifts of Healing
The Forgiveness Workshop
Dan Bird
Finding Your Way in the Spiritual Age
Waking Up in the Spiritual Age
Julia Cannon
Soul Speak – The Language of Your
Body
Ronald Chapman
Seeing True
Albert Cheung
The Emperor's Stargate
Jack Churchward
Lifting the Veil on the Lost Continent of
   Mu
The Stone Tablets of Mu
Sherri Cortland

Guide Group Fridays
Raising Our Vibrations for the New
   Age
Spiritual Tool Box
Windows of Opportunity
Patrick De Haan
The Alien Handbook
Paulinne Delcour-Min
Spiritual Gold
Holly Ice
Divine Fire
Joanne DiMaggio
Edgar Cayce and the Unfulfilled
   Destiny of Thomas Jefferson
   Reborn
Anthony DeNino
The Power of Giving and Gratitude
Michael Dennis
Morning Coffee with God
God's Many Mansions
Carolyn Greer Daly
Opening to Fullness of Spirit
Anita Holmes
Twidders
Aaron Hoopes
Reconnecting to the Earth
Victoria Hunt
Kiss the Wind
Patricia Irvine
In Light and In Shade
Kevin Killen
Ghosts and Me
Diane Lewis
From Psychic to Soul
Donna Lynn
From Fear to Love
Maureen McGill
Baby It's You
Maureen McGill & Nola Davis
Live from the Other Side
Curt Melliger
Heaven Here on Earth
Where the Weeds Grow
Henry Michaelson
And Jesus Said – A Conversation
Dennis Milner
Kosmos
Andy Myers
Not Your Average Angel Book
Guy Needler
Avoiding Karma
Beyond the Source – Book 1, Book 2
The History of God
The Origin Speaks

For more information about any of the above titles, soon to be released titles,
or other items in our catalog, write, phone or visit our website:
PO Box 754, Huntsville, AR 72740
479-738-2348/800-935-0045
www.ozarkmt.com

Other Books by Ozark Mountain Publishing, Inc.

The Anne Dialogues
The Curators
Psycho Spiritual Healing
James Nussbaumer
And Then I Knew My Abundance
The Master of Everything
Mastering Your Own Spiritual Freedom
Living Your Dram, Not Someone Else's
Sherry O'Brian
Peaks and Valleys
Riet Okken
The Liberating Power of Emotions
Gabrielle Orr
Akashic Records: One True Love
Let Miracles Happen
Victor Parachin
Sit a Bit
Nikki Pattillo
A Spiritual Evolution
Children of the Stars
Rev. Grant H. Pealer
A Funny Thing Happened on the
     Way to Heaven
Worlds Beyond Death
Victoria Pendragon
Born Healers
Feng Shui from the Inside, Out
Sleep Magic
The Sleeping Phoenix
Being In A Body
Michael Perlin
Fantastic Adventures in Metaphysics
Walter Pullen
Evolution of the Spirit
Debra Rayburn
Let's Get Natural with Herbs
Charmian Redwood
A New Earth Rising
Coming Home to Lemuria
David Rivinus
Always Dreaming
Richard Rowe
Imagining the Unimaginable
Exploring the Divine Library
M. Don Schorn
Elder Gods of Antiquity
Legacy of the Elder Gods
Gardens of the Elder Gods
Reincarnation...Stepping Stones of Life
Garnet Schulhauser
Dancing on a Stamp
Dancing Forever with Spirit

Dance of Heavenly Bliss
Dance of Eternal Rapture
Dancing with Angels in Heaven
Manuella Stoerzer
Headless Chicken
Annie Stillwater Gray
Education of a Guardian Angel
The Dawn Book
Work of a Guardian Angel
Joys of a Guardian Angel
Blair Styra
Don't Change the Channel
Who Catharted
Natalie Sudman
Application of Impossible Things
L.R. Sumpter
Judy's Story
The Old is New
We Are the Creators
Artur Tradevosyan
Croton
Jim Thomas
Tales from the Trance
Jolene and Jason Tierney
A Quest of Transcendence
Paul Travers
Dancing with the Mountains
Nicholas Vesey
Living the Life-Force
Janie Wells
Embracing the Human Journey
Payment for Passage
Dennis Wheatley/ Maria Wheatley
The Essential Dowsing Guide
Maria Wheatley
Druidic Soul Star Astrology
Jacquelyn Wiersma
The Zodiac Recipe
Sherry Wilde
The Forgotten Promise
Lyn Willmott
A Small Book of Comfort
Beyond all Boundaries Book 1
Stuart Wilson & Joanna Prentis
Atlantis and the New Consciousness
Beyond Limitations
The Essenes -Children of the Light
The Magdalene Version
Power of the Magdalene
Robert Winterhalter
The Healing Christ

For more information about any of the above titles, soon to be released titles,
or other items in our catalog, write, phone or visit our website:
PO Box 754, Huntsville, AR 72740
479-738-2348/800-935-0045
www.ozarkmt.com